FRAGRANCE OF A DEAD ROSE

A Reminder of Hope

Zaishah

Copyright © 2022 zaishah

All rights reserved

ISBN: 979-8422293414

No part of this book may be reproduced, or stored in a retrieval system, or transmitted in any form or by any means, electronic, mechanical, photocopying, recording, or otherwise, without express written permission of the publisher.

*You're
My
No. 1*

CONTENTS

Title Page	
Copyright	
Dedication	
Introduction	
You Are Enough	1
Memories	4
Holding On Is A Privilege	12
Sufferings	76
Choices	82
Trust The Timing of Your Life	95
Acceptance	109
thank you note	119
Books By This Author	121
fragrance of a dead rose iii	123

INTRODUCTION

You can't understand the beauty and value of love unless your heart falls apart. This book is a gentle reminder for anyone who is lost in life, experiencing difficulty in relationships, or searching for hope and trying to rediscover their self-worth.

No matter how hard life has been for you, no matter how tired you are, there's always a reason to live. There's always some hope amid the shattered pieces of a broken heart, just like there's some passion and love in the breathless bits of a dead rose, even after they've lost their beauty and all still smells great. Never ever give up on your life or your happiness.

This book will help those who are trying to heal from things they can't talk about.

YOU ARE ENOUGH

Life is not some kind of broken-winged bird that can't fly again. You must accept the fact that life is not guaranteed to be flawless or always wonderful. There is no such thing as a bad day, a bad moment, or a bad event that is expected to last a lifetime. Don't allow the things you can't control to define you. Or to turn you into someone who you are not. You don't have to achieve all your goals right now. You are not required to solve all the mysteries. It takes time for things to be clear. To unfold. And not everything you think is supposed to be great. Don't search for perfection in all aspects of your life. *Some things bloom better in their mediocrity.* Learn to live with the reality.

It's not that you shouldn't make any efforts; it's just that you shouldn't try to control or worry about things you don't have any control over.

> (EVEN IF WE GIVE OUR ALL, THERE ARE THINGS IN LIFE WE CAN DO NOTHING ABOUT)

Don't put so much pressure on yourself. You are exactly where you should be, even if nothing makes sense to you right now. Maybe you're not sure why this is happening to you. But you'll figure it out later in life and will realize why you had to go through it. And you will be proud of yourself. There's a reason for everything. It is not that you are asking too much, but maybe this isn't the moment. Maybe this period is set aside for you to recognize the potential to fight your battles alone. To teach you to believe in yourself. To instill confidence in you. Be patient. Keep your faith in the universe's ability to provide you with what you've asked for. The timing should be trusted. Trust gives you enough courage to fly, even in the haze of darkness and despair. It pulls you out of the state of utter confusion and disorientation and brings you back to life. Where there is no way, faith goes there.

MEMORIES

Suffering is a stage of life that everybody goes through, and we are no exception. It's not less than a tragedy that we have to live life without someone or something we can't even imagine being without. We are unable to do so due to a lack of bravery on our part. We believe that if this thing or person is not ours, we will most likely die, or that our lives will then be worthless. There will be no meaning to our existence. In a nutshell, our entire world is made up of that one person. Time, on the other hand, moves at a breakneck pace and spares no one. Autumn blankets the bright spring days. Within the haziness of dark nights, the bright light of day blurs. Whatever catastrophe befalls us, it draws us into its fading supremacy. It happened so quickly that we are unable to assess the extent of the destruction or to focus on what is left for us. But one thing remains that reminds us that we were once connected to them. With what was left after this heavy blow, regardless of how short the time was, the important thing is that we were with them and that they truly loved us with all of their hearts. Memories.

❖ ❖ ❖

The bridge that reconnects us back to time and takes us to what we have left behind.

Sometimes it takes a long time for us to realize the value of moments. But by the time we figure out how much they are worth, they are gone. Sometimes we are so busy making the moment perfect that we don't remember to focus on living within that moment. And other times, we get so involved in the moment, in things, in places, with some type of connection or with a person that we almost forget that nothing can be taken for granted. We forget that everything has an end, and one day this will undoubtedly come to an end as well. Perhaps we know the consequences, but we don't want to recall them. Perhaps we are afraid of reality, and we prefer to forget it. Perhaps we are simply afraid of endings because we know, somewhere deep within our hearts and minds, that nothing can last forever for us. We know there is an over in f**ore**v**er**. We know that sooner or later, this will no longer be a part of us, but we don't want to squander or risk losing the moments that we have in our hands by worrying about the time or events that are yet to happen. We understand that this, too, will end, but *we tend to be reluctant to accept and admit how things work, how* *they melt away.*

◆ ◆ ◆

Memories are all that will remain.
A familiar scent, an old song, a very cosy little chat, a blurry photo, some vintage stuff, a romantic poem, a whirl of closeness or a unique sensation takes no time to remind us of the memories of special moments when we are part of something bigger than ourselves. We get caught up in the past, remembering good old times and people who are no longer with us. It is not important whether they lost sight of us or whether we got separated from them along the way. But the fact that memories cannot be erased or eroded by the passing of time is important. We have no choice but to own them. No matter how good or bad they are, or how much they hurt or make us feel lost, we all love to remember old things. Memories are gone moments wrapped in the coat of sensory triggers and particular experiences that are sparked by the same stimulus in the future and evoke an emotional response within us. The past is part of our DNA. It reminds us of where we came from and how far we have come. What we have lost and what is left for us. *We own nothing but what we don't have anymore.*

Replaying the past in the present

Isn't it wonderful that a fleeting moment that cannot be recreated can be catalogued in the back of our heads and we can keep it with us for the rest of our lives? That's how things go in general. Everything around us changes, but memories remain untouched. Time flies, but it doesn't delete the past. They stay tuned with us. Memories are evidence of our existence. At the end of the day, all we have are some fixed and secure moments. They find a way to make a home for themselves within us and settle down in our midst. They know how to live forever. Apart from what is left behind, everything dies. Some moments wait for the right moment to be realised by us. However, memories are painful when the person for whom and with whom they were created is no longer present. Despite knowing that holding the past in the present will do nothing but damage us, we don't care at all. The only thing that matters to us is not to forget them and never let go of the memories of those who don't belong to us anymore. We may not be able to change how things end, but we still have a way to keep them alive. We still hang on to the things we once loved and lived in. Though they are gone, they will always be with us, because there's a reason for it. And every reason finds its way to manifest itself. They are worth keeping and are destined to be protected. It is a simple way to take care of things that we do not risk losing at any cost.

Take me back to the time when pain was unknown to me and my heart didn't learn to ache. When I thought, no matter where life took us, the thing between us would never change. When I used to believe in the concept of forever and assumed that all would be the same. When I used to believe in you. Take me back to those times where we didn't have to pretend to be strangers. Where we weren't you and me. Where we used to be us.

Why were we meant
to cross paths
if we were strangers
before and
we are
strangers
now?

Please take me back to the days *when I had all of you*. I wish you could be here. I wish you always loved me or didn't love me at all from the start. I wish you were not lost. I wish you had never let me go. I'm tired of missing you. But I don't want to spend any single second in my life in which I can't experience the pain that rips across my heart and soul, reminding me of how empty my love was that you didn't notice it. It hits me like a hot rock that I have never been enough for you. I wasn't the kind of person you needed. Yes, I am tired of missing you. But I don't know what I would do if I stopped myself from feeling the presence of emptiness that you left for me. There is no reason to forget about you. No reason not to miss you. Some people are worth missing.

At the very least, in a world where I am not deserving of having you all, I have something that belongs to you and binds me to you.

(I HAVE SOME OF YOU, AT LEAST)

HOLDING ON IS A PRIVILEGE

It was an honour for me to have you.
Those nights with you are the most heartfelt and secure I've ever experienced. The days I spent in your possession were truly magical. The flowers you brought for me are still fresh in my room. Those seasons when you held my hand in yours will always be with me. I can still sense your touch. I still remember those moments when you loved me for the first time. The gentle caress of your lips can still be felt all over my body. My hair can still feel your fingers moving through it. My pillow still smells like you. The echo of your footsteps is still striking the chords of my heart. Your graceful tone, hazel eyes, warm smile, pure heart, melodic voice, every part and every inch of your body are still vivid in my mind. I still have a strong sense of your presence. You are wherever I go. Everything is in the right place, except for one thing. You. The thing that is missing is you. And your absence is enough to throw everything into chaos. You're the time of my life.

(I WISH I COULD PAUSE THE TIME BEFORE THE PAST)

Before I met you,

I have no idea what's wrong with me. I really had no intention of falling in love with you in the first place. Yes, I love you. And I don't know why. I don't know when and how it happened to me. How you happened to me? Yes, I'm in love with you but don't know what to do.

(SERENDIPITY)

I used to wonder how people fall in love. What makes them believe they can't live without that one person? How can they not unlearn someone's name in their entire life? How come they can't find someone else in the world with a population of 7.9 billion people? How do they find it difficult to forget one particular person even after meeting dozens of people daily? I used to wonder that before I met you.

(EPIPHANY)

Whenever
I see
you,
my
heart
almost
forgets
to
beat.

(EUPHORIA)

You're

making

me

believe

I can't

live

without

you.

(HIRAETH)

I loved you without knowing the meaning of it. I loved you without any reason to love you.

> (I LOVED YOU WHEN I DIDN'T EVEN KNOW HOW TO LOVE)

The
excuses
I
invented
for
loving you
are
more
solid
than
the
justifications
you
have
for
not
loving
me.

Sometimes we are so into a person. Despite knowing they are not good for our souls; we give them more than they deserve. Deep down, we know someday they will break us so badly, but we repeatedly and intentionally ignore everything and every thought that goes against them. And one day, they show us why we shouldn't.

Keep

me

where

your

heart

is.

I want to know how it feels

to be a part of you.

Don't look at me with the look of love
if you are not actually in love with me.
Because you will pretend,
but I will fall in love

-with a deception.

(HYGGE)

I don't think about you.

You
make
me.

You are the one for whom I broke all my rules. For the first time, I stopped being hard on someone. For the first time, I let someone cross my boundaries. For the first time, I chose to give someone a chance, and that someone was you. Because I knew there would never be another like you. Just to keep you in my life, I broke all my rules.

(IS IT OK IF I TELL YOU THAT I LOVE YOU?)

You're the kind of person that I used to see myself falling in love with. The one I have read about in classic poetry and romance books. My eyes search for you when you are not around. I can't make myself stop thinking about you. I need you like I need air to survive. Your smile, your eyes, and everything you do make me fall in love with you. I may fall in love a billion times, but always with you. You are the sun that makes my life brighter. When you are with me, everything seems beautiful. When I look into your eyes, I see a home there. I feel safe in your possession. When I am in your arms, I forget every pain. You have made my life so complete and so meaningful. I want to walk beside you till the end. Because I don't know how to walk through life without you. I don't know how I'd live without you.

(YOU'RE THE PERSON OF MY DREAMS)

You're effortlessly amazing. You deserve all the greatness in the world. And I'm afraid that I'm not the one. I'm not that great. I love you. And I want to be a person who can give you everything wonderful this world has to offer. I want to love you in all those ways you want to be loved. I want to be the person on your mind. And one day, when I've turned into the person who you truly deserve, I will ask you to be all mine, for a whole life time. With the hope that when I come to hold your hand, I will find all the doors to you open. But, until then, could we please just be friends?

(SO, WILL YOU BE MINE FOREVER?)

It was all in the eyes

It was always in the eyes,

what he never saw,

what I was never able to say.

In
a
world
full
of
worries,

you are my moment of happiness.

I once heard your voice
and have never been able
to forget its sound.

(I WANT TO HEAR IT FOR THE REST OF MY
LIFE)

FRAGRANCE OF A DEAD ROSE

I'm falling for you
without any intention of it,

      (THE WAY RAIN FALLS ON THE EARTH)

When I saw you

for the first time,

I never came back

from that moment.

When I don't know
what it is like to be
in
love,
how could I resist
falling for you?

(AND EVEN IF I KNOW, WHY WOULD I DO THAT?)

I don't know
how
to
think
like
I'm not in love with you.

You are the moon to my earth,
and I have never been able to reach you.

> We didn't say it,
> we just felt it.

(We got scared. scared of falling in love _____we lost it all in the fear of attachment, rejection, abandonment, thoughts of not being enough or too much, in the idea of protecting ourselves.)

> (AND IN OUR EFFORTS TO AVOID HURTING EACH OTHER, WE END UP BREAKING OUR OWN HEARTS)

I want to share a part of me with you that I'm scared of sharing with myself.

(MERAKI)

If loving you is not a good idea, I would love to be ruined by you. If loving you is not wise, then I must confess that, I am insanely in love with you.

(INEFFABLE)

I want to be with you. Not because of your looks, or for your money, or your status, or anything else. I want to be with you because it is just all I want. It's everything to have you here.

(AND THAT'S IT)

I'm torn between
I can
live
without
you,
and
not
wanting
to.

I Love you for you. Because you never pretend to be who you are not. Do you know why I like you? You did not lie to me, not even when you had a chance. You knew that you would lose me by telling the truth. But you chose to tell me the reality instead of making excuses and covering yourself up.

You never tried to impress me. Not a single time.

(AND THAT WAS ENOUGH TO MAKE MY HEART FLUTTER)

ZAISHAH

I never felt___ I never felt anything wild like you. You are so weird, and you know what is weirder than that? I like weird.

My heart will always be your home. No matter when you return, you will find the doors open. There's no one else who deserves this place. This was meant to be yours from the beginning. Either you or no one. I will keep it safe for you. If I have to wait for you for the rest of my life, no matter if you return or not, I will. Because you are worth waiting for.

(YOU HAVE MADE ME KEEP MYSELF RESERVED FOR YOU)

The warmth
of your
eyes is
worth

skipping
a beat
for.

(EVERY TIME I SEE YOU, I WISH I COULD SEE
YOU ONE MORE TIME)

Although the distance between us is greater than the space between the skies and the earth, and more than the vastness of the ocean, I can still hear you in the rhythm of my heartbeat. You can be out of my sight, but you can't get out of my mind. *I miss those days when we used to be us.*

(HEARTLESS LOVE, KNOCKING
FROM THE INSIDE)

ZAISHAH

I was so into you that I never found time to think about what I would do without you. That's why I'm still holding onto your memories, because this is all I know. Because this is the only place where l can have you.

(THIS IS WHERE I'M AT)

>
> Once
> upon
> a time,
> there was
> you
> with
> me.

(AURORA)

ZAISHAH

And when he asked me to give him
a single reason to stay,
I was not even able to say
I needed him
the same way
the earth needs the sun.

You didn't just leave me;
you took me along with you.

(I'M HOMELESS WITHOUT YOU)

I won't be able to love again because I don't want to feel anything for anyone else that l once felt for you.

    (YOU'RE THE FULL STOP OF MY LIFE)

FRAGRANCE OF A DEAD ROSE

I used to believe
forever was an illusion

and then you said goodbye.

You were never there;
it was just me.
It makes me feel hurt that

there was never an us.

Could you please
 stay for me
and
 never
let
me
go?

But all I was asking for was you.

There are always some people in our lives with whom we cannot afford to be angry for a long time, no matter how unfairly they treat us. We forgive them, even if they don't feel sorry for what they have done to us. We repeatedly give them chances. We can't oust them from the place they hold in our hearts. We can't undo our feelings for them. We can't unlove them. We really want to be a part of their lives and don't even care where they put us. We can't risk losing them at any cost. Because we don't know what we'd do without them.

> (NO ONE ELSE IN THE WORLD CAN GIVE OUR HEARTS THE KIND OF BEAT THEY DO)

In the

desire of

getting you,

I think I lost you.

I
loved
you
even
when
you
didn't
make
any
sense
to me.

>   Before
>   you
>   say
>   goodbye,

will
you
be
mine?

I was never important for you to not let me go. You didn't love me much to keep me.

            (I WISH I MATTERED ENOUGH TO YOU)

This was the first time I thought you would be different from everyone else, because you made me believe that. This was the first time I decided to give my all to someone, but you proved me wrong.

> (YOU NOT ONLY LEFT ME, BUT LEFT ME ALL EMPTY)

I may be hard to love. Or maybe I want you to make sure that you're the one before I give my all to you. Maybe I am scared because I don't know what true love means. Or maybe I'm tired enough of dealing with people and know very well that they are not who they pretend to be. Maybe I'm not afraid of commitment so much as I am of being with the wrong person. Maybe I'm afraid of falling in love with someone who only loves the idea of a person. Or maybe I love you, but I'm afraid you'll leave my heart broken, just like every other person I've tried to keep in my heart. Maybe I love you, but I'm unwilling to admit it for fear of not being loved by you.

What if it is

not what it is?

what if it is

just a

weak moment?

> I make bad decisions,
> and I don't want you
> to be one of them.

(I can't love you because love hurts. It shattered you to pieces. And takes away everything. Because when two people who were once in love give up on each other, they lose it all. *I don't want to lose you at any cost.*)

Leaving me was your choice,
and loving you blindly
is mine.

(CHOICE)

You speak to my heart

I will never love another
the way I loved you,
because there's no one
as weird as you're.
And there will be no one.

(IRREPLACEABLE)

The space between us was
like the space between

the moon and the sun.

(UNREACHABLE)

It was meant
to be permanent.
But you didn't give
 it a *chance.*

(THERE IS NOT ENOUGH COURAGE IN THE WORLD TO FALL IN LOVE)

I wasn't important enough to you that you didn't bother to say final goodbye to me. It kills me to the soul that I was never deserving of our last goodbye.

(UNSAID GOODBYE)

Maybe we were just
meant to see ourselves fall for each other,
like two separate banks of a river,

never to meet.

Love was not wrong; timing was
Your earth was in a different galaxy,
my moon was in a different sky.

(OCEAN IN BETWEEN)

It was all a matter of choice. You were the only one on my list, and I was nowhere on yours.

(PRIORITIES)

Your avoidance doesn't prove you don't love me.
You definitely love me, but probably
not in the same way.

(ALONE IN YOUR ARMS)

You were
the sky,
and
I was
always

afraid to fly high.

One thing I don't like about love is that you don't fall in love by choice; instead, love chooses you. And once you are in love, there's nothing you can do about it. You can't change how you feel. Every time you see them, you start falling for them in a new way, stronger than before. You start to find more reasons to keep them in your life. You want to see them, talk to them, hang out with them. You can't convince yourself that everything here is okay and there's no need to worry about it.

You know you're messed up, but there is no way out.

I loved you enough to fight for you no matter what.
And more than enough to let you go for good.

In the space between
you and me,
there was love,

a lot of love.

You said you would always be there for me, but I didn't think in the shape of memories. I had no idea you meant seconds when you promised me forever.

I'm holding an insurmountable burden. I'm carrying the weight of pain that can't be carried. Sometimes it is intense, sometimes it is vivid, but it never goes anywhere. It doesn't fade away. I don't ever think it'll ever stop hurting me.

(WAITING FOR YOU TO COME BACK)

SUFFERINGS

Both pleasure and suffering are born in the heart. The more we care about something, the more we get depressed when it is gone.

(I've felt your absence with the same intensity with which I fell in love with you)

Some pains are meant to last forever.
The pain that no word will provide it with a vocabulary of expressions because that word has not yet been invented. The pain that no phrase has so far been formed to explain it. The pain that can't be written down because there's not enough ink in this whole world. The pain that no amount of bandaging will alleviate. The pain that is incurable and unending. The pain that is causing me to float like a speck of stardust. The pain whose burden cannot be carried by my shoulders.

The pain that is etched in my chest. The pain that aches in my heart. The pain that ripples across my body. The pain that has been trapped in my rib cage for forever, and the keys to which I have lost in my blood stream. The pain that runs through my veins. The pain in the colour of which my blood is stained. The pain reverberates in my ears. The pain that bleeds from my eyes. The pain that echoes in my head. The pain that gives flavour to my life. The pain that is eternal in this mortal existence. The pain that is holding me like love. The pain that doesn't concern with times and reasons. The pain that remains ever green through all seasons since it fed on my tears.

❖ ❖ ❖

The pain that leaves me feeling like I'm at the zenith of winter and keeps me cold all of the time. The pain that reminds me of autumn and makes me collapse to the ground as if I were a fallen leaf. The pain that lasts all day and night and burns me like summer. Every day in my chest, this pain flourishes like spring: it blooms, blossoms, and burgeons. The pain that has frozen in my heart like a hammer, and no one has dared to move it. The pain that keeps me dripping wet all of the time is like ocean.

That pain is as important for breathing as oxygen. Like memories, it is permanent. The pain that is as restless as the moon that keeps me awake all night. That is like roads that go nowhere. That is like a river destined to flow. The pain that is dark like the dead of night. That stays awake as if it were a day. That is deep like the sea. The pain that is like the sun that makes me feel it is not going anywhere. That is widening like the sky. The pain that I can't get away from since the world has no corners to escape. That is intense, similar to a storm. That is as mild as a breeze. The pain that defies all odds, like an impregnable fort. That is meant to stay forever.It has burned itself into my stomach. It is enveloping me within the thick of its robust roots. And absorbing my identity, and paralysing me. It is sucking me out of me.

I know this suffering is unending and unavoidable. My chest hurts. My heart aches. But this is all that I have left from your side. Even though it's hard and difficult, just like you. It is worthwhile because it belongs to you. It is my honor that I am destined to hold it. *It is a privilege for me to own it.*

(I owe you for this)

> A PART OF ME WILL ALWAYS WONDER
> WHAT IF I ASKED YOU TO STAY.

Some voids should be left unfilled.

Some cracks aren't required to be repaired. Some stains never go away. Some sights aren't worth-seeing. Some matters must remain unfinished and unresolved. Some questions need to be left unanswered. Some trails are not recommended. Some places should not be visited. Some leaves bloom to fall off. Some experiences are set up to fail. Some clouds don't condense for shower. Some houses are built to be abandoned. Some routes aren't good to take. Some highways are not designed to travel on. Some beginnings start to end soon. Some happenings are never supposed to occur. Some words are coined to hurt us. Some hearts are made to be broken. Some people come into our lives to leave us.

Some aches and pains are intended to be endured indefinitely. Some wounds and scares are forged to put on. Some stories are destined to be written. Some poems are written to read out loud. Some shattered pieces are worth being fixed again. Some connections are only to feel. Some things are there to be together. Some goodbyes live on forever. Some hearts are born to fall in love with. some hugs deserve to wait for. Some split seconds are worth delaying. Some memories will undoubtedly stay with us for the rest of our lives. Some losses will surely never be remedied. Some endings will never end. Some unfulfilled desires will always remain a dream. Some faces will never be forgotten. Some untouched moments between us will forever be remembered. Something that went unspoken between us will surely never go down.

AND EVEN WHEN THEY ARE OUT OF SIGHT, SOME THINGS DO NOT GET BLUR.

CHOICES

The *"path"* we take in the critical moment of now or never make or break our lives.

The moment of *"or"*, the moment of *"if"*, the moment of *"whether"* defines us who we are. The moment when we can't decide whether we should move on or stay here. Whether we are in the right place or need to be somewhere else. Whether we are doing our maximum or are capable of more. Whether we should walk with the crowd or just follow our natural flow. Whether we need a break or everything here is alright. Whether we are enough for ourselves or want more. Whether we should give up on somebody or try one more time. Whether we should give them a chance or not, at all.

The strength of our character is measured by such moments where we seem unable to reach any decision or make a choice. The validity of all real-life experiences is demonstrated by the decision taken at that moment. *It's not always about making the right choice; it is more about how well we can endure the consequences of a wrong decision.* We can't always make the best choice. And when we try to do so, we are denying reality. This is naturally unacceptable. So, when you're at a fork in the road, make the best decision you can. *Choose wisely.*

Success is all about taking the right turn at the right time. Tell yourself that all the turning points in your life are going to change everything you belong to. You can make a shambles out of it, or it could be a once-in-a-lifetime opportunity. Depending on how you handle the situation, it might be a disaster or a chance you've been looking forward to for a long time. You can screw it up, or you can seize the moment. It's all up to you.

It could be the moment when you have to decide to change your job or your city. It could be the first time you fall in love, the realization that you need to tell someone how you really feel about them, or when you find out you're pregnant. It could be when you see your best friend is becoming distant from you, or when you discover your partner is cheating on you, or a break up. It could be an accident that results in the loss of your health, or when you get diagnosed with some serious disease, or the sudden collapse of your business, or an academic failure, or the death of your beloved ones. It could be anything, from your work to your family, from your academic to your practical life, that has the power to shatter you into thousands of pieces and alter your life's destiny. What you choose at that time either makes you or breaks you. You either succeed or learn some lessons. There will be a change in your personality and perspectives. You won't be the same person as you were before.

And when you need to take a turn, take the right turn. This is the one and only chance to do something, to make a big difference. There is no such thing as a third option. You can't afford to spend your entire life stuck in the middle of a crossfire between heaven and hell. You deserve a safe place for your heart and mind. You have to find some way out of all this deadlock. You deserve a haven. Life, on the other hand, doesn't really operate in a vacuum. You must make the call.

The route life wants you to take might be hard for you to follow sometimes. But you have to go on because this is the only way to move forward. Because the winding journey and rolling roads usually bring comfort at the end. Not all life stages can be our favorites. We need to sometimes read a stupid chapter to carry on with the storyline. Things that contradict our hopes and wishes often prove the best one for us. So, every time in life when you are asked to decide, you should go for the best decision possible. It is not about what is easy; it's more about what's right. It is about what the proper thing is. *There is a difference between what is right and what is easy. Choose what is right for you, and work hard to make it easy.* Even though you don't want to go that way, you have to, because it is exactly what you need.

Life is worth living for

And then comes the time in our lives when the earth seems to have been yanked from under our feet. The sky has crashed down with all of its might on our heads. We're on our knees. And there's nowhere for us to go. Because it had been too late by then. The time when we feel that the path, we have been following all our lives was wrong from the beginning. When we have a nagging suspicion that something isn't quite right. When we have the feeling that our decision was not the best one. The point at which we know we've been trapped in a hall of mirrors with no way out. The point where we believe there is nothing left to do. When we are drenched and intoxicated with fears of remorse. When we begin to suffocate under the shadow of an amorphous, unnamed fear. But we forget that we still have a life to live ahead of us.

Retake sovereignty over your boundaries and borders. Reclaim hold of yourself. And once you've made your decision, stick to it. Take responsibility for your choice. Your decision has its own set of consequences. Own them. Sadly, we make poor decisions the majority of the time. Scrutinize your past experiences. You'll realize that you have made a bad call 70% of the time. In some people's lives, this ratio may be as high as 80%. So, there is no reason to be scared if you mess this up or fail to reach the right decision. After all, there are situations we may learn from. There are experiences that educate us. And experience mostly comes from poor decisions. It is a universal principle. Don't you think so?

You can't learn anything from a book that simply shows you how to make a decision in real life or what choice would be best for you. Until you put it into practice. You won't improve, and you won't be able to improve, until you've been in this phase. Books can't teach us what we learn from a decision, particularly from a wrong decision that we make in our practical life. Books can only teach us when we do what they want us to do. When we begin to act on the lessons that books are trying to teach us rather than just reading them, we learn. When we read them with the intention of improving ourselves and applying their insight to our lives, we grow. Books, of course, instill in us a sense of conscience and wisdom. However, we gain experience from our daily lives.

Don't let a stupid call ruin your life. If you've done the wrong thing, you should benefit from this too. So, you don't fall into that trap again. Accept responsibility for your errors. Learn from them and improve yourself. Improve your ability to make good decisions. There's no need to sulk and cry, because there's no reason for it. It is foolish to try to ignore the mess you have created, since you believe that nothing can be done now. Or persuade yourself that perhaps that's how God meant things to be or that is what is written in your destiny. We can't spend our entire lives hiding behind the fence of these unworkable, silly remarks. What is the point of moaning? What is the use of lamenting your fate? Who will guarantee that if you do this, everything will go back to normal? Whining about something over which you don't have any control is just a waste of time. What you can do at that moment is accept the aftermath of what you have done. This is the only place where you will be safe. This is your home.

> CONCENTRATE ON TRYING.
> AND KEEP TRYING UNTIL YOUR
> DISAPPOINTMENT TURNS TO HOPE.

Perhaps what we consider to be incorrect today will turn out to be nature's best choice for us later in life. *Who knows what the future holds?*

Unless you know what is unhealthy for you, you can't choose what is good for you. Life is all about experiencing and learning. You don't get validity if you don't take any risk.

With the passing of time, everything fades away except for one thing: *the lesson.* Forget about the taste of pain, but keep in mind what it means. What it leaves unanswered. Unfinished. From where it fell.

TRUST THE TIMING OF YOUR LIFE

The world around us is continuously changing. Never lose sight of what's most important to you.

Things fall apart to show you what is really important to you. Never forget that difficult situations make you stronger. Every day, life teaches something new, something different. Things that are meant to stay in your life will manage to find a way. If it is written into your fate, it will happen anyway. Things that are in the right place have a way of sticking around in the long run. They will never be taken away from you. You will never be denied what is rightfully yours. *And what is rightfully yours will find you soon, believe me.*

We all experience pain at some stage in our lives. Heartache and despondency are normal aspects of our lives. Some traumatic events or failures, or maybe a flash of insight that provokes us to pause and recognize our purpose in life: what we're here for. The meaning of our existence can lead to our suffering. Unexpected events, it is fair to say, add flavor to our lives. If everything goes on smoothly and works as planned, we may become bored with life. Of course, there are times when you feel lost, confused, or disoriented. But it is perfectly reasonable that things go wrong from time to time. Life does not always work in our favor. Sometimes we get sucked into the weeds, into the thick of thin things. Tough times and challenges hit us like a ton of bricks, and life throws us at the mercy of circumstances, leaving us shaking our heads and wondering, "What Happened?"

It's completely okay for us to have bad days. It's fine if you're stressed and sometimes succumb to several layers of pressing issues. After all, burying your emotions and suffering, failing to acknowledge them, convincing yourself that you're okay, or telling yourself that pledging for your emotions and pain is pointless will leave you debilitated and exhausted in the long run. We ought to make it a habit to look at things from a wider perspective and in the most constructive light possible.

We may have no control over what happens around us, but we do have control over how we react to it.

It makes a huge difference if you pay attention to what is going on with you and take it seriously. You've lived through a lot of traumas in the past, and you'll no doubt learn to cope with this one as well. Have faith in the universe. Believe that you will not be burdened with something you are unable to carry. There is nothing outside of your control in this world. Even the dreadful situation that is hurling you to the ground and cracking your bones isn't as tough as you are. Think in order to have faith in yourself. Keep your fingers crossed and hope that something positive is on the way.

It makes absolutely no difference what kind of heartbreak you've experienced. Draw valuable life lessons from challenging times. And never, ever leave yourself at the mercy of your plight. Time passes. Paradigms keep evolving. Things move. Relationships come to an end. People will certainly leave. However, life, on the other hand, goes on. If life does not stop for you, then why do you? Don't lose interest in things. Do not give up on life. Don't let one unpleasant experience, one rough day, one awful person, or one stupid decision define you. Learn to keep moving forward without pausing to look back in time.

All will fall into place and make sense. All will be back to normal. There is no such thing as **forever** in existence. It involves time for the body to recover properly. Healing takes time. Allow it a chance. Give it that time.

**SUFFERING IS WORTHWHILE
WHEN YOU OWN IT.**

You are more than Enough

At times when there is no one for you, you need to be someone for the sake of yourself. You must have faith in yourself. You must learn to listen to yourself. Sometimes all you need is to be brutally frank with yourself. To know who you are.

Why don't you open up to yourself if no one is there to hold your hand and tell you all will be fine? Why don't you put yourself out there for you? Why aren't you making yourself accessible to you? Hug yourself, speak positively to yourself, encourage yourself, and be your own best friend when life gets you down and affects you personally. Make a concerted effort to have faith in yourself.

At times, you need someone to acknowledge your efforts. At times, you need someone who reminds you of how valuable you are. You need love. You need someone to admire your presence. Someone who can tell you that you are stunning from the inside out. At times, you need attention. You need someone to reassure you that you are good enough for them. Someone to care for you. Someone who tells you that it's okay to be less than perfect. This is the person they need. At times, you need someone who takes you for a guarantee. When no one tells you that you are beautiful and worthy of love, you must love yourself and admire your beauty.At times, you need someone to understand your silence. At times, you need someone to make your surroundings worthwhile to live in. At times, you need to laugh wild with you. At times, you need someone to talk at 3: am just because you find it hard to sleep. At times, you need someone to count the stars with you just because you are feeling bored. At times, you need someone to dance with you in the rain on the street. At times you need to go for a long drive. At times you need to invest your time and feelings. At times, you need to create an everlasting flame of love. At times you need a weirdo like you.

> WHEN NO ONE IS WILLING TO MAKE TIME FOR YOU, YOU MUST MAKE TIME FOR YOURSELF TO ENJOY YOUR COMPANY.

At times when there is no one left by your side. When there is no shine from the sun to mask your darkness. When there is no hope for tomorrow. At times when wings alone are not enough to fly. When there's no more greatness in you. When there is no more passion and love left in you. At times when there is not enough air to breathe. When there is no way to go. When there is no home for you. At times when there is no choice for you. At times when there is no comfort zone in your life. When there is no shade in the sky. When there is no one to rescue you. When there is no empathetic ear. When there is no understanding heart. At times when there is no shoulder to break your silence. When there is no one to share your heavy burden with. At times when you've had enough of being strong and numb. At times when you find your pillow soaked in tears. When your soul is out of whack. At times when you are losing your stamina and sight to see things clearly. When things don't go as planned, and you find yourself alone with no one to stand by your side, or to hold your hand. At times when you simply need someone to be around you.

WHEN EVERYTHING SEEMS TO BE WORKING AGAINST YOU, YOU SHOULD WORK ON YOU. REMEMBER TO BE KIND TO YOURSELF.

At times when you can't escape, give up, or divert yourself from the emotional state you are trying to avoid. When you are desperate and there's no one to console you, to comfort you. When you get down in the dumps and there's no one to help you get out. When you need someone to lean on their shoulder to express what kind of pain you are experiencing. When you have had enough of listening to others, and you need someone to listen to you as well. When you need confidence, but you don't have someone to back you up. At times when you need someone to help you manage your frame of mind. When you need someone to share the darkness you carry. When you need someone to own you with your flaws. When you need someone to fix your problems. To bandage the scratches of your soul. To fill your lungs with positive vibes. To rebuild your faith in kindness. At times when you need to relearn how to breathe and walk again. When you actually want someone to help you. When you need someone to taste the pain of your tears, to know the scars on your soul, to talk about the story behind your reservedness____Clean your wounds. Allow your tears to dry before continuing.

WHEN THERE IS NO REASON TO BELIEVE IN HOPE AND YOU ARE AT YOUR LOWEST, PUT ON A PRETTY SMILE AND TRY TO SHINE ONCE MORE.

Sometimes you already have
what you're searching for.
Sometimes the radiance
you seek in others
is already
inside
you.

ACCEPTANCE

Not all suffering is worth enduring. Not all pain is worth hanging on to. It is a privilege. We should learn and figure out what is and is not worth suffering for. It is a privilege because we are not always chosen or given the opportunity to see the true value and color of things. You are worth appreciating because you persevered in the face of adversity, because you overcame hardship when you didn't feel you could.

There's a plan.

You've probably noticed that when we're out shopping, we see something we want to buy but don't have the funds to do so. We tell ourselves that we will save the money and purchase it later. However, the next time we go, it's out of stock: it's sold out. And we never get that. Life follows the same principle. We don't get all we want.

Sometimes we get the things that we desperately want when we have no passion for them. When we no longer care for them.

Likewise, certain things become a part of our lives but are still unimportant to us. They make every effort to keep in touch with us, but neither our hearts nor our minds are willing to open their doors to them to let them in. We don't take them seriously. We also have no place in our lives for them. Even if they, by chance, become a part of us, we will never be able to give them the value they really deserve. But it's too late by the time we realize we didn't treat them well. And we are left with nothing but regrets.

Time has a way of teaching us what is important to us and what is not. What is and is not meant for us. Sometimes we find what we're searching for all the time in our entire life when we're not interested in it anymore. Or sometimes we realize later in our lives that this is not the thing we wanted to have.

We don't always succeed in achieving our goals. We don't always get what we want. Sometimes we get what we need to have. I think it is necessary for us to know *the difference between our wants and needs.*

Sometimes the things we've spent our entire lives looking for are right in front of us all the time. But we seem to be unfamiliar with the idea of them, with the definition of possession. We seem to be unable to make sense of them. We seem to be unaware of their existence. We never embrace them. And they go unnoticed by us. It is not that we can't see them. Not because they are too subtle to notice, but because we are not ready to accept them. We are unwilling to carry them. We make the mistake of undervaluing them. *We underestimate what we have and chase after the unattainable, losing sight of what we're seeing in the process*. We do not seem to be ready to carry the weight of light and simple things. Perhaps we think there must be something wrong with what we are getting so easily. Perhaps we haven't yet managed to develop the habit of appreciating things that are easy to carry. Things that hold zero weight. Of the kind that we receive without having to put forth any effort. We have yet to build up the aspiration to embrace things. We still have no idea how to value something. How to hold it until the end of time.

Some doubts are clear. We learn to not to believe in them. Some fears are paper triggers. We learn to withstand them. Some realities can't be changed. We learn to accept them. Some views are so panoramic. We learn to limit them. Some intimacies are espoused. We learn to oppose them. Some seasons never elapse. We learn to ignore them. Some truths are bitter. We learn to swallow them. Some commitments are fallacious. We learn to flout them. Some damage makes a mess of us. We learn to award them. Some consequences are pernicious. We learn to draw wisdom from them. Some lessons are easy to remember. We learn to unlearn them. Some memories are unforgettable. We learn to erase them. Some ideas are up to scratch. We learn to fail them. Some dreams are absurd. We learn to give them a try. Some nights are insomniac. We learn to be okay with them. Some possessions are necessary. We learn to skip them. Some feelings are real. We learn to avoid them. Some people are worth remembering. We learn to forget them. Some records are chronicled. We learn to lose sight of them.

Some roles are disgusting. We learn to bear them. Some stories are anecdotes. We learn to leave them behind. Some passions are permanent. We learn to let them go. Some doors are closed. We learn a way to open them. Some opportunities are unavailable. We learn to make them in stock. Some things are resistant. We learn to penetrate them. Some things are inevitable. We learn to live without them. Some houses are hunted. We learn to live within them with readiness. Some tasks are difficult. We learn to carry them. Some moves are repetitive. We learn to diffuse them. Some events don't make sense. We learn to relate to them. Some nostalgia and souvenirs are regrettable, but we eventually learn to never mind them.

Some wounds don't heal, and we learn to underpin them. Some pains don't go anywhere, and we learn to endure them. Some feelings are poisonous, and we learn to let them thwack us. Some mistakes never change, and we learn to absorb them. Some shadows linger indefinitely, and we learn to keep them intact. Some routes are out of the way, and we learn to bypass them. Some trips are without a destination, and we learn to roam freely. Some relationships are demanding, and we learn to invest in them.

Some scenes make us lost, and we learn to let them distract us. Some serendipitous moments are breath-taking, and we learn to value things out of the ordinary. Some decisions are undone and we learn to own them. Some answers are unknown, and we learn to keep them locked. Some paths lead nowhere, and we learn to leave them.

Some feelings are periodic, and we learn to ignore them. Some situations are out of our control, and we learn not to resist them. Some things are not meant for us, and we learn to give up on them. Some goodbyes are silent, and we learn to feel them. Some tragedies are very expected, and we learn to tolerate them. Some opportunities wait for us, and we learn to take advantage of them. Some suffering is self-seeking, and we learn to move on.

Some injuries go deep, so we learn to bandage our soul. Some darkness lasts forever, so we learn to grow with a glow. Some squalls are ravaging, so we learn the value of peace. Some moments are hard, so we learn to smile. Some attitudes towards us are toxic, so we learn to admire kindness. Some efforts are fruitless, so we learn to be patient. Some downfalls tear us apart, so we learn to rise again. Some grievances are extremely personal, so we learn to go alone. Some connections are challenging, so we learn the validity of commitments.

◆ ◆ ◆

Some beauty is so fragile that we learn to protect it. Some journeys are arduous, so we learn to fly boldly within the haziness of misery. Some expectations are overwhelming, so we learn to secure our personal space. Some things go wrong, so we learn to wait for what is right for us. Some breaks are mandatory, so we learn to get out of our current mental state and perceptions of life.

Some dispatches leave us speechless, so we learn to use our heart strings. Some tears are overloaded, so we learn to trust in our strength. Some endings are relentless, so we learn that not everything is worth starting. Some efforts are not maximum, so we learn to do more than maximum. Some days are bad, so we learn that tomorrow will never be the same as today. Some failures are loud, so we learn to mute them. Some things can never be ours, so we learn to acknowledge their absence. Some dreams don't come true, so we learn how to chase after them.

Some gratitude takes time,
so we learn to notice them.

(GIVE YOURSELF SOME TIME, EVERYTHING
WILL BE OKAY)

THANK YOU NOTE

Dear Reader,
Thank you so much for purchasing and reading my book. I am extremely grateful and hope you found value in reading it. I hope that it added at value and quality to your everyday life.

Please consider sharing it with friends or family and leaving a review online. Your feedback and support are always appreciated, and allow me to continue doing what I love.

If you enjoyed this book and found some benefit in reading this, I'd like to hear from you and hope that you could take some time to post a review on Amazon. Please go to (https://www.amazon.com/Fragrance-Dead-Rose-Reminder-Hope/dp/B09TZ6TJF1)

love,

You can follow the author on instagram @zaixhah

BOOKS BY THIS AUTHOR

All Is Not Lost: Journey To Yourself

Every single step you take forward, no matter how insignificant it may seem, is significant. No matter how small your daily progress may be, it all adds up in the end. Keep going, going, and going until you're proud.

Standing and waiting for the storm to end won't end it unless you decide to go through it and face it.

This book is a collection of prose with a soft poetic touch. It will help you understand what it means to keep moving forward in life, and it will remind you of the strength that lies within the broken pieces of yourself. It will take you on a journey to discover self-love.

It talks about how to rise again after a fall. Always keep in mind that no one will come to save you. No one comes. It's you. It's always you who gets this power.

Fragrance Of A Dead Rose 2: Beauty In The Broken

This book is a collection of prose with a soft poetic touch. It's a gentle reminder that no matter where you are in life, you are not alone. If you're struggling with life and trying to find your way, this book will give you hope, inspire you to move forward, and help you reconnect with yourself.

Roses may die, but their delicate fragrance lingers on. Similarly, just as there is always something to be grateful for in life, there is also always some reason to keep going.

Sometimes life takes you in the exact opposite direction than you had planned. Slowly but surely, someday you will be okay again. Have faith; pain only makes you stronger in the end.

FRAGRANCE OF A DEAD ROSE III

coming soon

Printed in Great Britain
by Amazon